2nd Violin

For String Quartet or String Orchestra
Arranged and Edited by Joanne Martin

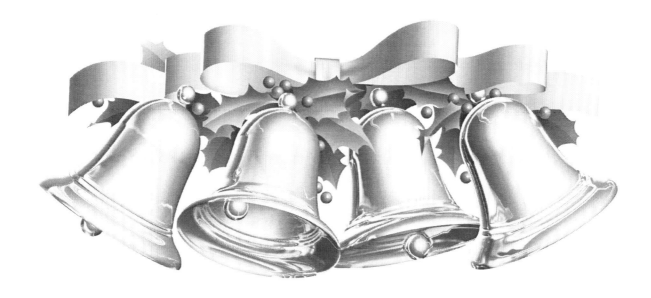

Copyright © 1998 Summy-Birchard Music
division of Summy-Birchard Inc.
exclusively distributed by
Alfred Publishing Co., Inc.
All rights reserved   Printed in U.S.A.

ISBN: 0-87487-987-6

CONTENTS

INTRODUCTION

The holiday season is a time of festive gatherings, and the music of this time of year is especially well-loved. There are many opportunities to play with multi-generation family groups, as well as mixed level studio and school ensembles. *Festive Strings* is a collection of well-known Christmas and Chanukah melodies in arrangements which have evolved to meet the needs of the individuals, groups, and orchestras I have taught. In order to provide maximum flexibility, the collection is available in a number of instrumentations:

Festive Strings for String Quartet or String Orchestra
      Appropriate for: Suzuki students in Book 4 and beyond
                           Middle school or high school orchestras

Festive Strings for Violin Ensemble
Festive Strings for Viola Ensemble
Festive Strings for Cello Ensemble
      For 2, 3, or 4 violin, viola, cello players in any combination of these instruments
      Appropriate for: Suzuki students in Book 4 and beyond
                           Middle school or high school orchestras

Festive Strings for Solo Violin
Festive Strings for Solo Viola
Festive Strings for Solo Cello
      For use with: *Festive Strings for String Quartet or String Orchestra*
                        Festive Strings for Violin, Viola, or *Cello Ensemble*
                        Festive Strings Piano Accompaniments
      Appropriate for players with 1–4 years of experience

Festive Strings Piano Accompaniments
      For use with: *Festive Strings for String Quartet or String Orchestra*
                        Festive Strings for Violin, Viola, or *Cello Ensemble*
                        Festive Strings for Solo Violin, Viola, or *Cello*
      Appropriate for intermediate level pianists

Christmas and Chanukah tunes are popular with students at all levels, and even the youngest beginners enjoy taking part. With this in mind, I have chosen the most accessible keys, which usually are the most resonant keys for string players. Occasional compromises were necessary because of the differences between the violin, viola, and cello.

Introductions are optional and may be used at the discretion of the director or performers.

Shifting is kept to a minimum, and finger numbers are normally used only to indicate the first note of a new position. Occasionally, notes which remain in position are marked in parentheses.

In *Festive Strings for String Quartet or String Orchestra*, the melody is passed around so that all members of the ensemble can have the opportunity to play the tune. Score and parts are marked with "Melody" and "Harmony" to help players bring out the melody at the appropriate moment.

These orchestra arrangements can be played by a string quartet; the instrumentation is complete without the bass part. For the most part, Violin 3 duplicates the Viola part; where the parts are different, the Violin 3 part appears in small notes in the score.

"Jingle Bells" appears in both D Major and A Major. The D Major arrangement is less demanding technically, while the A Major gives a brighter sound. When these arrangements are used to accompany less experienced players, I recommend using the A Major version with violinists and the D Major version with violists or cellists.

During the preparation of this collection, many colleagues, friends, and students have played the arrangements, and their advice and detailed suggestions have been invaluable. In particular, I would like to thank Alex Adaman, Joanne and Charles Bath, Carey Cheney, Sally Gross, Eric Hansen, Carolyn Meyer, Rick Mooney, Karla Phillipp, Robert Richardson, Patricia Shand, Carol Tarr, and Ruth Wiwchar. *Festive Strings* is dedicated to my husband, Peter, in gratitude for his incredible patience and constant support.

I hope that you enjoy *Festive Strings*, and that these arrangements contribute to your enjoyment of the holiday season.

                                                                                Joanne Martin

TEACHERS' NOTES

Jingle Bells in D Major

Violin 1 melody in chorus 1
Viola melody in verse 1
Cello/bass melody in chorus 2
Violin 1 melody in verse 2
Violin 2 melody in chorus 3

Violin 1 shifts to D (third position)

To facilitate page turns, *Festive Strings for Violin, Viola, or Cello Ensemble*; *Festive Strings for Solo Violin, Viola, or Cello*; and the *Piano Accompaniments* use a D. S. al Fine for the last chorus of "Jingle Bells" in D Major.

In *Festive Strings for String Quartet or String Orchestra*, the last chorus of "Jingle Bells" in D Major is written in the parts.

Joy to the World

Violin 1, Violin 2 melody in verse 1
Viola, Violin 1 melody in verse 2

All parts are in first position

Chanukah

Cello/Bass melody in verse 1
Violin 1 melody in verse 2

Bass shifts to D (third position)

Away in a Manger

Cello/Bass melody in verse 1
Violin 2 melody in verse 2

Bass shifts to D (third position)

Jolly Old Saint Nicholas

Viola melody in verse 1
Cello/Bass melody in verse 2

All parts are in first position

God Rest Ye Merry, Gentlemen

Unison, Violin 1 melody in verse 1
Viola, Violin 2 melody in verse 2

All parts are in first position

S'Vivon

Viola, Violin 2 melody in verse 1
Violin 1, Cello/Bass canon in verse 2

Cello shifts to E flat (second pos.)
Bass shifts to D (third position)

S'Vivon is the Hebrew word for a wooden top (dreydl) which is used in a traditional Chanukah game.

Jingle Bells in A Major

Violin 1 melody in chorus 1
Viola, Violin 1 melody in verse 1
Violin 2 melody in chorus 2
Violin 1 melody in verse 2
Violin 2 melody in chorus 3

Violin 1 shifts to D (third position)

To facilitate page turns, *Festive Strings for Violin, Viola, or Cello Ensemble*; *Festive Strings for Solo Violin, Viola, or Cello*; and the *Piano Accompaniments* use a D. S. al Fine for the last chorus of "Jingle Bells" in A Major.

In *Festive Strings for String Quartet or String Orchestra*, the last chorus of "Jingle Bells" in A Major is written in the parts.

Lo, How a Rose

Violin 1 melody

All parts are in first position

O Christmas Tree

Viola, Violin 1 melody in verse 1
Cello/Bass, Violin 2 melody in verse 2

Bass shifts or pivots to C
(second position)

Festive Strings for Violin, Viola, or Cello Ensemble; Festive Strings for Solo Violin, Viola, or Cello; and the *Piano Accompaniments* are written with one verse with a first and second ending.

In *Festive Strings for String Quartet or String Orchestra*, "O Christmas Tree" has two verses.

JINGLE BELLS
in D major

James Pierpont
Arranged by JOANNE MARTIN

Violin 2

JOY TO THE WORLD

Violin 2

George F. Händel
Arranged by JOANNE MARTIN

CHANUKAH

Violin 2

Traditional
Arranged by JOANNE MARTIN

AWAY IN A MANGER

Violin 2

Martin Luther
Arranged by JOANNE MARTIN

JOLLY OLD SAINT NICHOLAS

Violin 2

Anonymous
Arranged by JOANNE MARTIN

GOD REST YE MERRY, GENTLEMEN

Traditional
Arranged by JOANNE MARTIN

Violin 2

S'VIVON

Violin 2

Traditional
Arranged by JOANNE MARTIN

Violin 2

JINGLE BELLS
in A major

James Pierpont
Arranged by JOANNE MARTIN

LO, HOW A ROSE

Michael Praetorius
Arranged by JOANNE MARTIN

O CHRISTMAS TREE

Traditional
Arranged by JOANNE MARTIN

Violin 2